# TOP TIPS: INSPIRING ALL KINDS OF LEARNERS

Andy and Claire Saunders

© Scripture Union 2010
First published 2010
ISBN 978 1 84427 395 9

Scripture Union England and Wales
207–209 Queensway, Bletchley,
Milton Keynes, MK2 2 EB, England
Email: info@scriptureunion.org.uk
Website: www.scriptureunion.org.uk

Scripture Union Northern Ireland
157 Albertbridge Road, Belfast, BT5 4PS
Website: www.suni.co.uk

Scripture Union Scotland
70 Milton Street, Glasgow, G4 0HR
Website: www.suscotland.org.uk

Scripture Union Australia
Locked Bag 2, Central Business Coast Centre, NSW 2252
Website: www.scriptureunion.org.au

Scripture Union USA
PO Box 987, Valley Forge, PA 19482
Website: www.scriptureunion.org

All rights reserved. No part of this publication may be reproduced, stored in a retrieval system, or transmitted in any form or by any means, electronic, mechanical, photocopying, recording or otherwise, without the prior permission of Scripture Union.

The right of Andy Saunders and Claire Saunders to be identified as authors of this work has been asserted by them in accordance with the Copyright and Patents Act 1988.

British Library Cataloguing-in-Publication Data. A catalogue record of this book is available from the British Library.

Bible quotations have been taken from the Contemporary English Version © American Bible Society. Anglicisations © British and Foreign Bible Society 1996. Published by HarperCollins Publishers and used with permission.

Printed and bound in Singapore by Tien Wah Press Ltd

Logo, cover design, internal design: www.splash-design.co.uk
Internal illustrations: Colin Smithson
Typesetting: Richard Jefferson, Author and Publisher Services
Advisers: Alison Hendy, John Marshall

Scripture Union is an international Christian charity working with churches in more than 130 countries, providing resources to bring the good news of Jesus Christ to children, young people and families and to encourage them to develop spiritually through the Bible and prayer.

As well as our network of volunteers, staff and associates who run holidays, church-based events and school Christian groups, we produce a wide range of publications and support those who use our resources through training programmes.

# CONTENTS

| | | |
|---|---|---|
| Introduction | | 4 |
| Part One | What the Bible says about learning | 5 |
| Part Two | Some learning principles | 10 |
| Part Three | Equipping learners in practice | 19 |
| Ten Top Tips | | 31 |
| Resources | | 32 |

# INTRODUCTION

We have two daughters. When the younger one was three years old, she touched a light bulb and burnt her finger. We comforted her, the tears subsided – and then she touched the light bulb again! Asked why, she replied, 'I wanted to see if it always hurts!' She has continued to apply this learning principle again and again – test things out, experiment, and see what happens.

Our elder daughter, however, is very different. Faced with the prospect of a new task, she likes to do all the research first. This means she prefers to begin a project with as much information at her fingertips as possible. She is a confident user of Internet search engines!

Perhaps the most important lesson our daughters have taught us over the years is this: they are both utterly unique – as God intended. One way this uniqueness is manifested is in the ways in which they learn – and we ignore this at our peril.

This is an important lesson for anyone engaged in teaching children and young people. We want to inspire them, allowing them, not just to know their Bible, but to know God – and to do it in the way that suits them best. This book celebrates the uniqueness of every child whom you encounter. You will be equipping them to learn that the message of the gospel transforms lives.

We dedicate this book to Emily and Anna, who have taught their parents so much, in so many different ways.

# PART ONE – WHAT THE BIBLE SAYS ABOUT LEARNING

## General principles

### We are all unique
Time and again the Bible makes it clear that each person is uniquely made in the image of God (Genesis 1:26). Each of us is an individual because of our racial origin, family background, gender, language, likes and dislikes – and learning preferences. Some of this uniqueness is in our genes, and some is the result of nurture. God knew us before we were even conceived (Psalm 139:13–15). Each individual, therefore, matters to God and is invited to respond to him, in whatever way they can. This includes children and young people. If for no other reason than this, those of us involved in nurturing the faith of children and young people are called to recognise the wide range of ways in which they learn about and also respond to God.

### We are to know Jesus himself and not just know about him
In 2003, Mark Griffiths wrote a book on children's ministry entitled, *Don't just tell cute stories, Change lives!* You don't have to read beyond the title to know this book is about teaching and learning in a Christian context. The question at its heart is: do we want to teach our children and young people Bible stories that are worth knowing or to teach them about God who is worthy of their belief, using these stories?

How we answer this question will determine what teaching and learning activities we choose to use. The end result will either be children and young people who *have knowledge about God*, or children and young people who actually *know God himself*. This is a vital message, central to our approach to the task of teaching. Such a developmental and dynamic process involves both leader and child or young person in becoming more like Christ and thus being transformed. 2 Corinthians 3:18 gives us a glimpse of God's priorities: 'So our faces are not covered. They show the bright glory of the Lord, as the Lord's Spirit makes us more and more like our glorious Lord.'

### We are all called to obey and teach

Followers of Jesus are to be prepared to introduce others to God. In Matthew 28:19,20, Jesus commands his disciples to, 'Go to the people of all nations and make them my disciples.' But he did not stop there. He commanded them to teach others 'to do everything I have told you'. That's a tall order, but it is the starting point. Followers of Jesus are to teach God's Word, primarily as found in the Bible, because that's where we learn what God has 'commanded us'. This command comes with an encouragement too, as Jesus said, 'I will be with you always, even until the end of the world.' What's more, we are to share what we have seen and experienced of Jesus. This is a message worth sharing!

## How God teaches in the Old Testament

You may recall a learning experience when a teacher stood at the front of the class imparting information to a group of learners. Some in the class will have absorbed at least some of that information, but some will have taken in nothing! But that is only one way to teach and learn. Teaching and learning experiences can and should be much more varied and active than that. God himself did not stick to one way of communication and instruction.

**Think about…**
Reflect on your own experiences as a child at school or in a Sunday group. How much did you learn in both places? What helped you to learn?

Learning through experience is a powerful way to learn. When Abraham travelled to the region of Moriah in Genesis 22, he was obeying God's instruction to present his son Isaac as a burnt offering. This was testing Abraham's faith to the absolute limits, and yet he spoke with utter confidence when he told Isaac that God would provide a lamb for the burnt offering (verse 8). What he learnt through that experience was life-changing. His faith must have increased tenfold when God did indeed provide the sacrificial ram.

When Ezekiel encountered God (Ezekiel 1–3), it was a truly multi-sensory experience that left him in no doubt of the glory of God! The highly visual descriptions of the four living creatures are overwhelmingly strong and colourfully choreographed. It's hard to imagine a more vivid, dramatic or multi-sensory encounter!

Both of these episodes, and countless others, point to the principle that we should engage all of our senses as we learn more about God for ourselves, and share him with others. We are commanded to love the Lord our God with all our heart, soul and mind (Matthew 22:37). Learning was never intended to be a purely academic exercise! It is all about life, but that is no excuse for intellectual laziness!

> **Think about…**
> Look up Ezekiel 1–3 and note down all the strongly descriptive words used to describe what Ezekiel saw and experienced such as 'sparkling like ice', 'glowing like hot coals'. What different learning experiences do they describe?

## How Jesus teaches in the New Testament

Throughout the gospels we encounter the different ways that Jesus taught people; on their own, in small groups or in vast crowds.

### Role-modelling and training

For three years he lived with his disciples. He showed them what it meant to be fully human. He showed them who God was by the way he lived his life and died his death. He did not just talk to them, he discussed with them. He entrusted them with the task of preaching the good news, and mentored them. He was not going to let them get stuck in a rut in their learning and experience of him. All children and young people learn through observing their leader's behaviour.

### Using questions and conversation

Jesus was a brilliant storyteller and discussion group leader! For example, in Luke 10, when he told the story of the good Samaritan, passive listening was not an option! He ended by asking a question that echoed the original question that prompted the parable: 'Which one of these three people was a real neighbour to the man who was beaten up by robbers?' This was not the answer his audience expected.

Jesus' skilful questioning and comments can be seen in his conversation with the Samaritan woman in John 4 or when he challenged his disciples to declare who they thought he was (Matthew 16:15). From then on, Jesus began telling his disciples what would happen to him and their understanding expanded further. In his conversation with the two disciples on the road to Emmaus he gradually opened up the Scriptures and they suddenly understood (Luke 24:25–33).

### Using drama

The Last Supper could arguably be the most significant and poignant piece of acted-out truth that has ever taken place. Despite Jesus' explanation his disciples remained puzzled even though as Jews they had some understanding of the place of Passover celebrations (Matthew 26:26–29). The Last Supper event has been remembered by millions ever since. Other examples include Jesus feeding large crowds as he re-enacted the role of Moses giving out manna (John 6:5–15,32,33) or riding into Jerusalem on a donkey (Matthew 21:1–11) or washing the feet of his disciples (John 13:4–20). His disciples and the crowds observed, experienced, remembered and tried to make sense – all part of the learning process.

## Engaging and developing learners

Howard G Hendricks in *The Christian Educator's Handbook on Teaching* noted that 'a problem-solving mentality pervades the pages of the gospels. Jesus does not merely solve problems *for* people but *with* people; they are always involved in the process.' Jesus encouraged people to become engaged or indeed actively involved as he shared parables (eg the lost coin – Luke 15:8–10), demonstrated signs (eg John 2:1–10), used illustrations (eg Matthew 19:13–15), and offered direct challenges to step out in faith (Matthew 14:22–33).

Howard G Hendricks writes: 'Mark the results of Christ's teaching: amazement, fear, silence, belief and violent opposition, but never indifference or neutrality. Lives changed because his teaching objective provided not merely information but transformation.' Of course, we should never forget the role of the Holy Spirit in taking the teaching of Jesus to transform lives (John 14:26).

If our teaching provokes any of these responses, we will have moved beyond telling 'cute stories' to a place where lasting transformation is possible.

## 2 PART TWO – SOME LEARNING PRINCIPLES

### Different learning styles

Understanding how children and young people learn helps us be more effective in what we do with them week by week. Most people, whether consciously or subconsciously, tend to teach in the way that they themselves prefer to learn. However, if we only teach according to our own preferences, we risk not meeting the needs of a significant percentage of those in our group who learn in different ways from us.

One of the simplest ways to describe the different ways people like to receive information is to talk in terms of Visual, Auditory and Kinaesthetic preferences (VAK).

- **V**isual learners gain most from learning activities that involve seeing and reading.
- **A**uditory learners prefer listening and speaking.
- **K**inaesthetic learners learn best when given the opportunity to touch and do.

It is widely believed that around 20% of people are visual learners, 20% are auditory learners which leaves 60% of people as primarily kinaesthetic learners. (A chart to use with your team to identify preferences is on page 25.)

#### Think about...
How would you choose which new car to buy? Look at photographs and the model specifications in the brochure, listen to the opinions of others, or let a test drive be the ultimate decider? Your preferred method says something about how you approach learning.

A Sunday children's group might look something like this:
> You read aloud the first few verses of a Bible story before asking for volunteers to read. You then talk about the story and, at the end, you recap with a quiz to see how much everyone remembers. Hannah can't remember the story. (She couldn't even sit still whilst it was being read aloud, and her concentration wandered throughout!) Jess announces she preferred last week's activity, when she followed the text and there were pictures on the screen to bring the story to life. Alex has really thrived as he read his part with expression and enjoyed the variety of voices of other readers. He answers the most quiz questions correctly.

What made life easy for Alex was the presentation of the task itself. It suited his auditory learning preference. You might assume that Hannah is naughty or a fidget because she can't sit still. But she probably has a kinaesthetic preference and would have remembered lots more if she'd been involved by acting out the story in some way. Jess meanwhile is not being awkward but has missed out because she responds to what she sees – on the screen, in the Bible, with drama – and there was none of that this week.

## Different intelligences

The psychologist, Howard Gardner, (an Internet search will give you information about him) has developed a theory of multiple intelligence that challenges the long-held view that intelligence is fixed and can be measured by an IQ test. This is controversial, but Gardner's work embraces the whole person. His basic principle is that everyone possesses all of these types of intelligence to a certain degree, but will have greater strengths in some more than in others. He identifies at least seven types of people who might display these characteristics:

- Linguistic: communicates and makes sense of the world through language (poets and writers)
- Musical: performs, composes and appreciates music, with a heightened response to intonation and the rhythm of voice (composers)
- Logical-mathematical: uses and appreciates abstract concepts and offers a logical analysis of problems (scientists, mathematicians, philosophers)
- Spatial: perceives and transforms visual or spatial information (architects and engineers)
- Bodily-kinaesthetic: uses all or part of the body to create products and solve problems (athletes, surgeons, craftspeople)
- Interpersonal: understands other people and works effectively with them
- Intrapersonal: is self-aware, knowing their own emotions, desires and fears, strengths and weaknesses, and reacts appropriately to them

This brief summary of Gardner's work illustrates how people have intelligence and learning preferences that are defined in different ways. Traditionally, our culture has valued visual and auditory approaches to learning above the kinaesthetic, and essentially valued linguistic and logical-mathematical views of intelligence. Schools do now offer many opportunities to learn through doing and activity, but the evidence still points to a system that values listening, reading and writing above all else. Many students are left with the impression that some ways of learning are more acceptable than others.

**Think about…**
Does your church judge others (not just children) by the way they learn? Some adults are quite dismissive of other adults' learning styles. We must work towards toleration, understanding and appreciation.

## Passive and active learning

The distinction between passive and active learners applies to all learners, whether they are visual, auditory or kinaesthetic. Passive learners simply receive the material presented to them, without question. An active learner, however, will engage with it, making connections with what they already know or have experienced and asking questions to make more sense. It's not difficult to see why an active learner would be more likely to make sense of and remember what they have learned. How can we encourage this approach to learning, especially as it equips children and young people to make connections between what they have learned of God from the Bible with what is going on in their own lives? What we do with fresh information determines whether learning takes place, and transforms us from passive into active learners.

> **In reality…**
> Siobhan listened to the story of Jesus riding into Jerusalem but she was not curious about what was happening. Sam, however, was full of questions, especially as his uncle owned a donkey and he often went to watch football in a crowded stadium!

Take the imaginary example of the new mobile phone you have just purchased. It is a different make to your old one so you need to discover how it works. How you tackle this task indicates the way that you like to learn, which is your preferred learning style. There are many different theories on learning styles but one of the most widely accepted is the work of Honey and Mumford who have broadly identified four different categories. Let's take each of these categories and see how each applies to discovering how your new mobile phone operates.

- The **theorist** reads the instruction manual in detail to work step by step through the process of learning to use the phone. Theorists prefer to think things through in rational, logical steps.
- The **activist** embarks on a process of trial and error, experimenting with all the functions of the phone until they get it to work. They probably become frustrated if they can't make sense of it quickly. Activists like immediate results and enjoy a challenge.
- The **reflector** makes sense of the phone through observing it in use or perhaps listening to someone as they demonstrate it. Reflectors like to take a step back, gather relevant information to be sure they know what they are doing before they try for themselves.
- The **pragmatist** considers all options, and then decides on what they think will be the most effective way to learn how the new phone works. Pragmatists are problem-solvers who make practical, quick decisions.

> **Think about...**
> One outcome of active learning is that teachers must not be afraid of what seems like repetition. Have the confidence to tell the story, sing it, act it, paint it and then have a quiz on it!

Successful learners may have a preference for one particular style, but they are able to draw on a number of styles in order to learn, remember and apply new information. If we can design our teaching sessions so that children and young people draw on each of these styles, we can enable deeper learning to take place. Everyone is actively involved and no-one is excluded.

Active learning means that we learn through experience. We don't simply hear, see or do. In addition, we consider fresh information, turning it around in our minds like a tiny object in the palm of our hands. We then make decisions on the relevance of the information from what we have discovered or observed.

> **In reality…**
> Karl made a good innkeeper when the group acted out the story of the good Samaritan. He was surprised at how much the guests in his hotel disliked the stranger who brought in the almost-dead traveller. That set him thinking about how one unpopular boy in his class had shown God's love to a new boy.

Hearing a Bible story and remembering it will not automatically make sense to our own lives. We need to ask questions and puzzle about what it might say about God, how it might fit into the bigger picture in the Bible and how it might impact choices, relationships, attitudes and emotions. This increases the possibility of the kind of transformational learning that we considered on page 5.

## The Learning Cycle

Honey and Mumford's work was developed in studies by another theorist, David Kolb, who proposed a 'Cycle of Experiential Learning' (for details, visit www.businessballs.com). This learning cycle can help develop a structure for teaching that meets the needs of all learners. Marlene LeFever's work, which has been influential in Christian circles, is similar to this.

We can see how Kolb's Cycle works out if we return to our daughter's experience of touching the light bulb (see page 4). For her, touching the light bulb was a **concrete experience**. The rather painful **reflective observation** was that this action resulted in pain! However,

**Kolb's Cycle of Experiential Learning**

**Concrete Experience**
(doing / having an experience)

**Reflective Observation**
(reviewing / reflecting on the experience)

**Abstract Conceptualisation**
(concluding / learning from the experience)

**Active Experimentation**
(planning / trying out what you have learned)

Text and concept by Clara Davies (SDDU, University of Leeds)
Tutorial design by Tony Lowe (LDU, University of Leeds). Used with permission.

in order for this basic observation to become a significant learning experience, there was the need for some **abstract conceptualisation**, so that she could work out a general principle – if it hurt that time, will it always hurt? So, the general principle would be that a switched on light bulb will be hot enough to burn. A more experienced learner at this point may develop an alternative approach to test this theory, but in this case the **active experimentation** resulted in a second attempt at touching the light bulb! The **concrete experience** confirmed the theory: it hurt!

Let's see how we might use the same cycle of learning in a teaching session based on Daniel in the lion's den, by combining the work of Kolb and Honey and Mumford. You have decided that you want to explore the theme of trust, focusing upon Daniel's need to trust God, to be found in Daniel 6.

## Concrete experience

Introduce the theme of 'trust' linking it to the children's own experience and then help them to 'experience' the story of Daniel. Use some of the visual, auditory and kinaesthetic techniques mentioned earlier. This will also highlight the theme. Activist learners will benefit from this immediate experience to set the context of the session.

## Reflective observation

All learners need help to make connections between the Bible text and the questions about trust at the start of the session, but this is where **reflectors** will feel most at home. How would the children have felt if they were Daniel and knew that praying to God would be risky? Could they be certain that God would protect them? Was there not another solution for Daniel?

## Abstract conceptualisation

The session moves towards dealing with the **theorist** learners' concerns for how these biblical truths connect with real life. What possibilities do they open up for dealing with specific situations? By the time Daniel was pulled out of the den, what had he discovered about trusting God? We might not face such life-threatening situations, but what issues do we face where we see no easy solution yet believe that God can be trusted? By seeking answers to such questions from the text itself, we are allowing all learners to discover how the 'theory' of the Bible relates to their own lives.

### Active experimentation

The next stage is to try out solutions, apply principles, and ultimately change behaviour, becoming more like Christ. How are we going to be like Daniel, in practice? How do we show we trust God in the way that we pray? The **pragmatist** learners in the group will come to the fore here, suggesting ideas for trying out their learning in new situations – and it's likely the **activists** will want to try them out immediately!

It is worth remembering that Howard Gardner maintains that each of us possesses the different intelligences to different degrees, but given a favourable learning environment, anyone can strengthen all of them. A favourable environment is created by the use of sound, light, temperature and design, as well as practical issues such as the time of day the session takes place and whether the learners are hungry. External factors include whether learners work in groups, pairs or teams, and how they react to this, or whether they perceive the 'teacher' is happy for them to make mistakes and values different kinds of learner. All these factors contribute positively or negatively to the learning environment.

> **Think about...**
> What sort of a learning environment do you have in your services or groups? Is it a physically engaging building? Are all approaches to learning welcomed? What technology can you use to your advantage? With other leaders, create a checklist to see how you score.

# PART THREE – EQUIPPING LEARNERS IN PRACTICE

All children's and youth leaders are learners themselves. The first two parts of this book may not have connected easily with you because of how you learn. Part Three may feel more comfortable, but if that is the case, don't ignore the other two parts. Return to them after you have reflected on what you are about to read.

## Learning through all-age services

All-age services provide opportunities for everyone, whatever their age, spiritual maturity, abilities and family status to meet together to worship God using ways to learn and worship which are not usually expected in what is perceived as an 'adult' service. (This challenges leaders of adult services to think how far they are equipping *adults* to learn.)

Here are some of the elements of an all-age service that should be affected by the different learning preferences within a congregation. Scripture Union's *All-Age Service Annuals* and *Light for the Lectionary* resources are full of ideas you can adapt for different kinds of learners – see page 32 and the inside back cover for details.

Make sure that a team of people (which will include different learners) is involved in the planning and delivery of the service. This is time-consuming but is worth it because the service will be richer. There is scope for maximum involvement and usually it is OK for people to make mistakes and to learn from them. Build in plenty of variety and as people find they can worship God in ways that work well for them, they are more likely to accept (and even enjoy) elements of the service that are not explicitly geared towards their own preferences.

### Music
An all-age song is not necessarily a children's song and a 'kiddies' song is usually not an all-age one!

- Choose songs that have one theme.
- Some 'adult' songs may include difficult words and concepts or jargon phrases. This isn't a reason not to use them, but do take time to explain them. The adults might appreciate this too!
- Choose a variety of songs with good rhythms and strong choruses, quieter songs and even hymns. Outsiders with some Christian background will appreciate traditional hymns and songs.
- If you want people to join in, the tunes need to be singable.
- Use some action songs. Activist, kinaesthetic learners will probably love them. But some adults will not want to participate and there will be children who don't want to join in either. They may get just as much enjoyment from watching others do the actions. We want people to participate in ways that work for them, so never pressurise anyone to do actions!
- Encourage listening either to pre-recorded music or to the music group performing for everyone.

### In reality…
Our children chose 'Here I am to worship' and 'Indescribable' as songs to use in an all-age service. They had heard them on a CD in the car – a reflective song, with simple words and one with a strong beat with some fantastically complicated words about God. Neither is specifically a children's song.

### Bible reading
God's Word should be central in any time of worship together. Ensure that all learners are able to access the Bible reading, which will necessarily involve presenting it in a range of different ways.

Is there time for people of all ages to find the passage in their own Bible or Bibles in the pews so they can follow it? Words on a screen are helpful but the individual reader cannot control how quickly their eyes follow the reading! Visual learners may not want to just listen, so it may matter that they can read for themselves. Does a strong narrative lend itself to dramatised reading, so that auditory learners benefit from a variety of voices? Can sound effects be added? Can the whole passage be presented as a drama, even if that means the text is not presented word for word from the Bible? Is there a video that tells the story?

More challenging is providing opportunities for kinaesthetic learners to be active learners. You could:

- Provide paper and pencil for them to draw some of the characters in the story on four blank faces, giving each one a face that expresses their feelings.
- Everyone can mould an object, person or event after the reading, using silver foil, but playdough will do.

**Drama**
Offer a drama for everyone to watch, or include audience participation. This can be anything from inviting people to come forward to take part or have key words and phrases that require a response from the 'audience' – a vocal response, or a particular action.

**Prayers**
They can be read by one person or a group. Times of prayer can introduce other approaches that engage a variety of learning preferences – such as visual images on PowerPoint. We can pray in groups, writing, drawing or acting out individual or group prayers. People can move around the church to visit prayer stations or collect objects, carry burdens or perform actions in responding to God. People can kneel, hold their arms out wide or lie prostrate on the ground

(there are biblical precedents). Different ways help both active and more reflective adults and children.

### Reflective moments

Being aware of learning styles may mean that there is a move away from traditionally quite passive worship services, attuned to the more auditory and visual learners, to services where everything is noisy and active. Reflectors and theorists may feel alienated! Whether we are reflective or active in our preferences, we all need time and space to think and respond. Find opportunities for all kinds of learners to reflect by sitting in silence, or listening to music or enjoying a combination of music and visual images.

### In reality…

Even reflective times can appeal to kinaesthetic learners. Everyone was invited to collect a small stone to take home, as a reminder of how Abraham built an altar. Walking to collect the pebble and the rough feel of it served as tactile reminders of the story.

### The Bible talk

All methods of communication are vital in helping people to understand Bible teaching. It is recommended that no activity in an all-age service should last more than seven minutes which is shorter than many sermons! Do you have one talk or two or three shorter ones? How much active involvement is there or visual stimulus?

Here is how you might apply the learning cycle to the Bible talk (see page 16). Begin with a 'theme setter' to introduce the key theme and relate it to experience. You are asking questions such as, 'Why does this theme matter? How does it connect with everyday life?' In a second section, unpack the Bible itself, asking, 'What did this mean at the time? What is the relevance of the information in this passage?' A third section can present the challenge and ask, 'So what?' To break the sermon up like this allows creative opportunities for varying presentation styles for different kinds of learners. Sometimes just telling a powerful Bible story will need no explanation and will speak for itself.

**Length of service**
Too long and minds begin to switch off, children become restless, parents need a break and many people are not used to concentrating for a long time! An all-age service should be less than an hour. Better to end with people wanting more and open to staying around for refreshments and chat – vital for developing relationships!

**Environment**
You may not be able to do much to change or adapt your venue which may be an old building with pews, or a light and airy school hall. But there are some things you can do, wherever you are. Is the temperature right (too cold in the winter and too hot in the summer)? Are chairs laid out in the best way for your purposes? (Check the sight lines.) Can you add banners and artwork to make the space visually appealing? Are friendly people (including children) at the door to welcome others? Different learning styles will mean that people have a variety of contributions to make in creating the right environment.

## Midweek and Sunday groups

Groups for children and young people take place on Sundays and midweek, after school, on Saturday or during the holidays, in cell groups or in larger groups. How much consideration do you give to the learning preferences of group members? For ideas on working with small groups, read *Top Tips on Leading small groups* (SU) – see the inside front cover.

### Take a look at your group

Relationships are vital for any work with children and young people. You probably know about their friendship groups, hobbies and families, for example, as these form part of general conversations you have with them. But do you know how they learn best?

There are many learning style questionnaires available on the Internet, some of which are extremely complicated but visit www.businessballs.com for an accessible one. These will give some indication of the learning preferences of individuals in your group, but also serve as a useful starting point for further discussion. Keep Howard Gardner's multiple intelligences in mind as you chat and observe your group as they engage in different activities. You would find it easier to do this with a co-leader. You will begin to see different intelligences emerge which will be valuable as you plan future sessions. Children and young people do talk about learning styles at school.

Use one of your team planning meetings to do a learning style questionnaire together and discuss the results. A simple VAK one is on the next page. Most of us prefer to teach in the way that we prefer to learn. If all team members are theorists, activist children and young people may struggle with the content of sessions! Balancing your team

> **In reality…**
> A busy church leader said, 'We found that introducing a variety of learning styles into our programme meant team members had more to offer.'

*Top Tips on Inspiring all kinds of learners*

# VAK Learning Style Questionnaire

Are you: a VISUAL learner – you prefer pictures and images; an AUDITORY learner – you prefer words and sounds; a KINAESTHETIC learner – you like to learn through being physically active.

For each question, note down which option best describes you at this time. Add up the scores at the end. To do this in more detail, visit www.businessballs.co.uk. *Note:* this is a very simple indicator of what might be your preferred way of learning.

**A  When spelling a word do you?**
1 See the word. 2 Hear or say the word to yourself. 3 Write the word out to see how it feels.

**B  When you remember things, do you?**
1 See pictures first. 2 Hear the sounds first. 3 See moving images.

**C.  When you are working, what distracts you more?**
1 Untidiness around you. 2 Noise. 3 Movement around you.

**D  When reading, do you?**
1 Make your own mental images. 2 Hear the characters talking. 3 Imagine the characters moving in the writing.

**E  Which do you prefer to help you learn?**
1 Written work (books / web pages) with lots of facts. 2 To be told things. 3 To be active in doing things.

**F  When talking, do you?**
1 Not want to listen for too long. 2 Like to listen and discuss. 3 Move your hands about as you talk.

**G How do you prefer to be thanked?**
1 To get a letter or card. 2 To have it said to you. 3 A physical hug or hand shake.

**H  Which would you say?**
1 I hear you loud and clear. 2 I see what you mean. 3 I've got the hang of that now.

Count up how many answers are 1 or 2 or 3. Then turn the page upside down.

If most answers are 1, you are most comfortable as a visual learner, most answers are 2, an auditory learner, or most are 3, a kinaesthetic learner.

with different kinds of learners and challenging the team to teach in ways that appeal to a range of learners could transform your sessions.

### The programme

Review your programme to see whether it includes something to appeal to all kinds of learners. Use teaching material that follows the learning cycle in its approach. Scripture Union's *Light* material is based on these principles, as are other published teaching schemes. Adapt activities, and even whole sessions, to address the particular needs of your group.

Remember you cannot meet the needs of every learner throughout a whole session every week. But lots of variety will communicate that the children's and young people's preferences matter to you. Becoming a more mature learner means being able to gain something from all kinds of learning experiences. Encourage people to work together and learn from each other.

Use your team's strengths in the same way, by pairing up those with different preferences to deliver different elements of a session. Look out for children who are not engaging – an alternative approach might help them get involved in a way that works for them.

Many of the approaches to an all-age service are equally applicable to a group setting that involves Bible teaching. Here are some other suggestions for engaging different learning preferences:

> **Think about…**
> As a team, recall what you have done over the last two months. What might have especially helped visual learners, auditory learners or kinaesthetic learners?

### Visual learners

- Use a DVD of the Bible story.

- Display key words around the room, with accompanying pictures (names of people, places and themes).
- Use puppets or PowerPoint presentations to enhance key elements of teaching. This is useful in telling a Bible story but puppets can be used in 'role play' situations too.

**Auditory learners**
- Present the Bible story as a TV or radio interview, with one leader interviewing another. The children can be witnesses.
- Music complements activities, creating appropriate atmosphere, adding sound effects to a story.
- Hot-seat an individual, cross-questioning them about their part in a Bible story.

**Kinaesthetic learners**
- Use movement appropriate to the theme. Use different parts of the room as you move from one area to another, using simple prompts to mark out each area, encouraging everyone to come on a journey with you through the story.
- Use children as 'actors' in the story, with simple actions to mime, or working in groups to present a short drama of one part of the story.
- Use craft, construction or art as a way of learning through doing. This provides opportunities to talk about the theme of the session as you work together, creating work to proudly display to others.

You may run larger events such as holiday clubs or Saturday events. These should contain many of the elements already suggested. Action-packed and fast-moving events will certainly appeal to many who come. But don't forget to include elements that allow time and space for different kinds of learners. Can you include quieter activities and

> **In reality…**
> One Sunday group leader said, 'Last week, a child told me they were fed up with doing craft every week.' Being aware of learning styles has helped me explore different ways to be creative other than craft.'

space to think, as well as some games that do not involve lots of running around?

As with the all-age service, think about the venue. External factors will affect how children and young people respond to teaching sessions. Is your venue as welcoming and exciting as you can make it? Is it a place where they feel secure and a place of fun?

## Challenging behaviour impacts learning

Different teaching and learning styles will not eliminate bad behaviour, but they can help prevent it. It's important to consider the causes of challenging behaviour to identify whether a change in approach might at least be part of the answer.

Challenging behaviour is not exclusively the responsibility of the child or young person themselves! They may just be tired, bored, find an activity difficult, just feeling out of sorts that day or they may suffer from ADHD. Ask a few basic questions of them or their carer and then take appropriate steps to improve the atmosphere for everyone.

### The session plan

Does it reflect the different learning styles you have identified in members of the group? Is there enough variety and pace to keep everyone interested? A classic opportunity for children to play up is during the transition from one activity to another. Make sure that at a time of transition, both the team and children know what is happening and expectations are clear.

The beginning of a session is when children are likely to be at their most alert and ready to learn. Make the most of this opportunity. At the end, give them a short time to think what they have learnt and then allow them to share their reflection with a neighbour. This helps to clarify their thinking and apply their experience in the session to life. Most children will be used to this because it is common practice in primary schools and increasingly used in secondary schools.

**Physical factors**
Children who arrive at an after-school club are likely to be hungry and this may result in bad behaviour. Can you provide some healthy, energy-boosting snacks to revitalise them? In contrast, children who arrive bright and early on a Sunday morning or at a holiday club may need to burn off energy before they settle down.

**Enough variety or choice**
Offer alternatives within an activity, so that different types of learner can engage in a way that suits them best. Children and young people like choice but sometimes you may need to make the choice for them.

Remember that those in your group come from a variety of backgrounds and with a range of educational abilities. Some may receive extra support for their learning needs in the classroom. Understand from the parents (or the young person themselves) what that support is and how it can be replicated in your programme. Putting in place some simple support strategies that enable a child or young person to successfully learn with their peers can avert challenging behaviour.

### Involving parents

Some parents feel that the education of their child is something provided for them by the school. They may not see that what you do with their child in a different context is something they are actively involved in. The Bible points to parents as those primarily responsible for a child's faith development. So it is important to see that we are working in partnership with parents. Particularly with younger children, find opportunities to chat with parents about how they feel their child is getting on. Ask questions about how their child seems to learn best. Parents' learning styles can shed light on a child's learning preference. Some ways of learning are genetic!

It is claimed that the average three-year-old's brain works twice as hard as an adult's brain! So much learning takes place before adolescence. No wonder more people come to faith in Christ before the age of 14 than at any other period of life. As children and youth workers we are privileged to provide the tools for children and young people to learn about and from God, learning in the ways that suit their own unique personality. The better the quality of learning, the deeper will be their relationship with him. Lives will be transformed.

### In reality…

A leader of a midweek club commented, 'One of our more challenging children was becoming calmer and more focused. This was because we understood his learning needs so much better after chatting to his parents and his school teacher who happened to live near a team member (but did not break professional confidences).'

# TEN TOP TIPS

Build relationships with your children/young people and the team.

Be more creative in your ministry by focusing on how people learn.

Set time aside to evaluate how children or young people are learning.

Don't worry if things don't always go as planned. Evaluate and try again! And don't try to meet every learning style in one session.

Remember the quieter child/young person.

Keep in mind that using different learning styles is a learning process for all involved.

Look for others beyond your team who may have fresh insights to share on learning.

Make the most of the first few minutes and at the end of the session encourage everyone to identify what they have learnt.

Encourage those engaged in adult ministry to explore the importance of learning.

Bear in mind that a disruptive or unsettled child may not be unintelligent or difficult, but maybe their learning style is not being catered for.

# RESOURCES

### Books to inspire
Margaret Cooling, with Ruth Bessant, Charlotte Key, *RE:thinking Book 2: Brain based learning*, Stapleford Centre, 2002
Kathryn Copsey, *From the ground up: Understanding the Spiritual World of the Child*, BRF, 2005
Mark Griffiths, *Don't tell cute stories – Change lives*, Lion Hudson, 2003
Bob Hartman, *Anyone can tell a story*, Lion Hudson, 2002
David A Kolb, *Experience as the source of learning and development*, Prentice Hall, 2003
Marlene LeFever, *Learning Styles*, Kingsway, 1998
Lucy Moore, *Messy Church*, BRF, 2006

### Resources
*Light* Scripture Union's curriculum material. See also www.lightlive.org, a free website of downloaded resources for Sunday and midweek groups
*All-age service annual Volumes 1–3* (SU) 2007, 2008, 2009
Sue Wallace, *Multi-sensory prayer* (SU) 2000
See inside front cover for details of the *Top Tips* series. Visit www.scriptureunion.org.uk for further details
*Pretty much everything you need to know about...series* on working with specific age groups.

### Websites
www.businessballs.com – lots of free resources
www.curbsproject.org.uk – CURBS, learning-based resources
www.godlyplay.org.uk – Godly Play, multisensory learning opportunities
www.messychurch.org.uk – Messy Church, intergenerational and multisensory learning
www.scriptureinion.org.uk/light and /eyelevel – a wide range of resources that acknowledge the different ways children and young people learn and engage with God.